Jurassic Blue

monstrous pieces for beginners

Caroline Lumsden and **Pam Wedgwood**

with illustrations by **Drew Hillier**

Contents

FABER *ff* MUSIC

Foreword

I hope you have as much fun playing these pieces as Pam and I had in the writing of them. Feel free to make them your own by adding second verse words where needed, inventing a new noise on the instrument, or trying out different dynamics. You can even create your own dinosaurs!

Caroline Lumsden

I really enjoyed drawing these pictures for you, but now it's YOUR turn to have fun and let your imagination run ... WWWWWILD! So go on, grab some pencils and fill the landscapes with your own imaginary dinosaurs—just as long as you remember to play your cello too!

Drew Hillier

© 2002 by Faber Music Ltd
First published in 2002 by Faber Music Ltd
3 Queen Square London WC1N 3AU
Music processed by MusicSet 2000
Printed in England by Caligraving Ltd
All rights reserved

ISBN 0-571-52199-1

To buy Faber Music publications or to find out about the full range of titles available please contact your local music retailer or Faber Music sales enquiries:

Faber Music Limited, Burnt Mill,
Elizabeth Way, Harlow, CM20 2HX England
Tel: +44 (0)1279 82 89 82   Fax: +44 (0)1279 82 89 83
sales@fabermusic.com   fabermusic.com

Scary, scaly Spinosaurus

1 Clap with words
2 Sing with note names

Ragtime ♩ = 116

mf Sca - ry, sca - ly Spi - no - sau - rus hunt - ing in a

pack. Clum - sy, hea - vy Spi - no - sau - rus, what a spi - ky back!

Search - ing for his e - ne - mies just who needs friends like that?

Sca - ry, sca - ly Spi - no - sau - rus; take care, watch your back!

Vicious Velociraptor

1 Clap with words
2 Play

Not too fast: count carefully – you might get eaten! ♩ = 92

f Vi - cious   Ve - lo - ci - rap - tor,   Vi - cious   Ve - lo - ci -

mp
-rap - tor,   Vi - cious   Ve - lo - ci - rap - tor,   vi - cious-ly kills   his

p
prey.   Yuk!   *mf* Grasp - ing the snout and   rip - ping the throat he

kills them with   a   jerk.   Flash-ing his tail   and   gnash -inghis teeth   a
pizz.
p Vi - cious   Ve - lo - ci -

arco
-rap - tor   you might get eat - en   for   his   *f* tea!

Which dinosaur is this?

Strong Iguanodon

1 Clap with words
2 Sing with note names

With strength and mystery ♩ = 104

f Strong I - gua - no - don, bold I - gua - no - don,

tear - ing down that huge tree. Strong I - gua - no - don, bold I - gua - no - don,

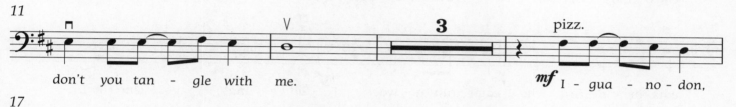

don't you tan - gle with me. mf I - gua - no - don,

I - gua - no - don, tear - ing down that huge tree.

f Strong I - gua - no - don, bold I - gua - no - don, spi - ky thumbs, let me be.

ff Strong I - gua - no - don, bold I - gua - no - don, don't you tan - gle with me.

* Think: 4/4 ♩ ♪ ♩ ♪ ♩
slow   quick slow   quick slow

... and how about this?

Plesiosaurus

on an idea by Alex

1 Play the rhythm 'plesiosaurus' across the D and A strings
2 Learn bars 14–21
3 Play bars 6–13 and 22–end

Sway with the breeze! ♩ = 100

Ple - si - o - sau - rus lives in the sea, he u - ses his flip - pers chas - ing his tea. He twists his neck quick - ly grab - bing his prey and eats lit - tle fish who can't run a - way! Glid - ing si - lent - ly,___ swift - ly through the sea. 'Scrump - tious lit - tle fish___

poco rit. **a tempo**

fol - low me!' Ple - si - o - sau - rus lives in the sea, he u - ses his flip - pers chas - ing his tea. He twists his neck quick - ly grab - bing his prey, and eats lit - tle fish who can't run a - way.

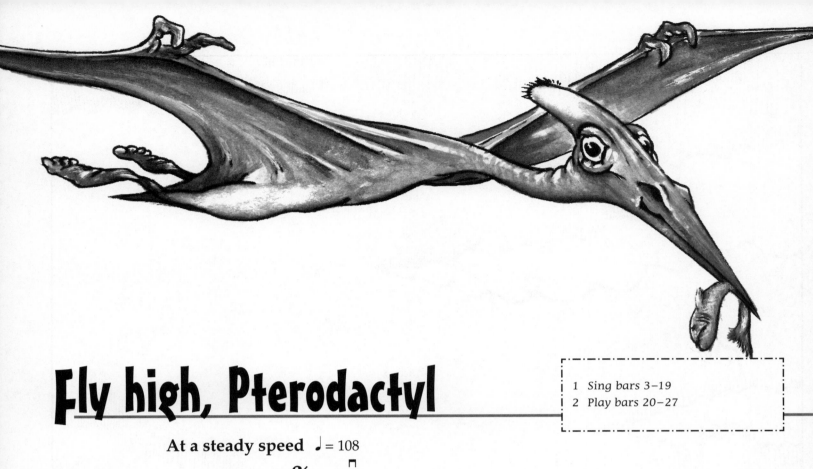

Fly high, Pterodactyl

1 Sing bars 3–19
2 Play bars 20–27

At a steady speed ♩ = 108

f Fly high, Pte - ro - dac - tyl, fly high with

me, fly high o - ver cliff tops, we'll reach the sea.

mp Fly high, Pte - ro - dac - tyl, with ti - ny feet,

f let's search for some din - ner, I'd like a treat, fresh

FINE

meat. *p* Fly high, flut - ter, flut - ter,

D. S. 𝄋 al Fine

f flut - ter, fly high, flut - ter, fol - low me.

Jurassic Blue

CELLO and PIANO

monstrous pieces for beginners

Caroline Lumsden and *Pam Wedgwood*

with illustrations by **Drew Hillier**

Contents

© 2002 by Faber Music Ltd
First published in 2002 by Faber Music Ltd
3 Queen Square London WC1N 3AU
Music processed by MusicSet 2000
Printed in England by Caligraving Ltd
All rights reserved

ISBN 0-571-52199-1

To buy Faber Music publications or to find out about
the full range of titles available please contact your
local music retailer or Faber Music sales enquiries:

Faber Music Limited, Burnt Mill, Elizabeth Way, Harlow, CM20 2HX England
Tel: +44 (0)1279 82 89 82   Fax: +44 (0)1279 82 89 83
sales@fabermusic.com   fabermusic.com

FABER *ff* MUSIC

Foreword

Jurassic Blue developed from working with children on the Beauchamp House Easter String Course 2000.

Following on from **Jackaroo**, these pieces start with a revision of the first finger and then introduce third and fourth fingers, as well as second finger and first finger extended back. The addition of words throughout means that all the pieces can be sung through first with the piano, and teaching points and a suggestion box for learning each new piece are given in the score. You may find the following formula a useful way to tackle a new piece:

1 Sing through once with the words

2 Sing and clap with the time names e.g. Spi-no-sau-rus (slow slow snap-py)

3 Sing and clap with note names e.g. BABD (♩ ♩ ♪♩.). Use 'effs' for F♯ and 'beef' for B♭

4 Finally, play!

With all the jazz rhythms found throughout this book, it is always much better to 'feel' them rather then try to be absolutely precise.

Versions of **Jurassic Blue** for violin and viola are also available, so that pupils can enjoy playing together. To give the viola and cello a better range, however, **Bony Stegosaurus** is in a different key from the violin version.

Finally, encourage children to make these pieces their own by adding second verse words where needed, inventing a new noise on the instrument, or trying out different dynamics. Ask them to write their own dinosaur pieces to encourage improvisation—they can even draw these into their part!

I hope you have as much fun playing these pieces as Pam and I did in writing them.

Caroline Lumsden

Teaching points

- Revision of first finger
- Understanding of 'snappy' rhythm (♪ ♩.)
- Simple string crossing

Scary, scaly Spinosaurus

Suggestion box
1 Clap with words
2 Sing with note names

Ragtime ♩ = 116

mf Sca - ry, sca - ly Spi - no - sau - rus

hunt - ing in a pack. Clum - sy, hea - vy Spi - no - sau - rus, what a spi - ky

back! Search - ing for his e - ne - mies just who needs friends like

that? Sca - ry, sca - ly Spi - no - sau - rus; take care, watch your back!

Teaching points
- Understanding of rests
- Up-bow anacrusis

Vicious Velociraptor

Suggestion box 1 Clap with words
2 Play

Teaching points

- Placing of third and fourth finger on the D string
- Syncopation

Strong Iguanodon

Suggestion box   1   Clap with words
2   Sing with note names

With strength and mystery ♩ = 104

Strong I - gua - no - don, bold I - gua - no - don, tear - ing down___ that huge

tree.   Strong I - gua - no - don, bold I - gua - no - don,

don't you tan - gle with   me.

Teaching points

- Placing of third finger on the G string
- String crossings
- Holding fingers down

Plesiosaurus

on an idea by Alex

Suggestion box

1 Play the rhythm 'plesiosaurus' *across the D and A strings*
2 Learn bars 14–21
3 Play bars 6–13 and 22–end

Sway with the breeze! ♩ = 100

Ple - si - o - sau - rus lives in the sea, he u - ses his flip - pers

chas - ing his tea. He twists his neck quick - ly grab - bing his prey and eats lit - tle fish who

can't run a - way! Glid - ing si - lent - ly,

swift - ly through the sea. 'Scrump - tious

little fish__ fol - low me!' Ple - si - o - sau - rus

poco rit. **a tempo**

lives in the sea, he u - ses his flip - pers chas - ing his tea. He twists his neck quick - ly

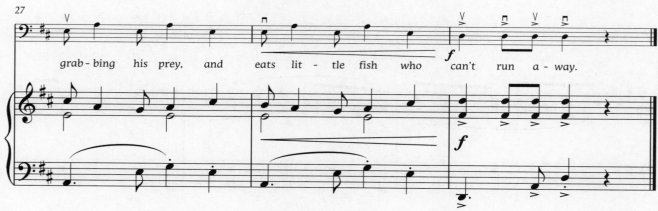

grab - bing his prey, and eats lit - tle fish who can't run a - way.

Fly high, Pterodactyl

Teaching points
- Placing of third and fourth finger on the A string
- Bow distribution
- Demonstration of (optional) trill

Suggestion box
1 Sing bars 3–19
2 Play bars 20–27

16

din - ner, I'd like a treat, fresh

19

FINE

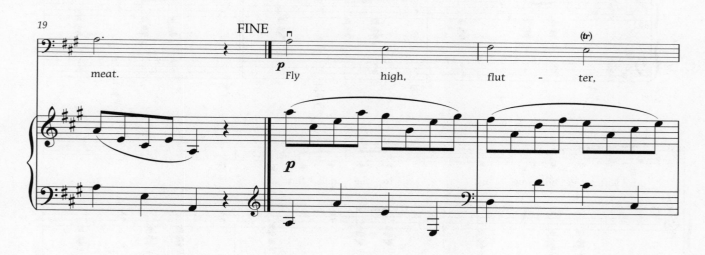

meat. *p* Fly high, flut - ter,

22

flut - ter, flut - ter, fly high,

25

D. S. ℅ al Fine

flut - ter, fol - low me.

Teaching points

- Placing of third and fourth finger on the C string
- String crossing
- Col legno and staccato

Bony Stegosaurus

on an idea by Matthew

Suggestion box
1 Sing and place fingers
2 Play

Spiky! ♩ = 104

Col legno

Bo - ny Ste - go - sau - rus,

do you think he saw us, is he look - ing at me?

Bo - ny Ste - go - sau - rus, what a di - no - sau - rus,

to Coda

don't you think we should flee?

Teaching points

- Confidence in singing
- Second finger on the A string
- Slurring in twos or a whole bar

Clever Compsognatus

Suggestion box

1 Sing
2 Play slowly with slurs in twos
3 Play using a bow to a bar (once learnt)

Cle - ver Comp - so - gna - tus, dain - ty Comp - so - gna - tus, don't take fright and run a-

- way. We could both be friends, I'd take you home to tea;

come to stay. Cle - ver Comp - so - gna - tus,

dain - ty comp - so - gna - tus, stay and play.

Teaching points

- $\frac{5}{4}$ time
- *Staccato*
- *Bow distribution*

Lazy Tyrannosaurus Rex

Suggestion box
1. Sing
2. Play bars 13–20
3. Play bars 5–12

Relaxed ♩ = 132

Triceratops Rocks

on an idea by Phoebe

Teaching points
- 'Quicker' rhythm (♩ ♫)
- Swing elbow

Suggestion box
1 Sing and clap
2 Learn bars 10–13 and 22–26
3 Play

Let's rock 'n' roll ♩ = 116

14 | arco | Tri-ce-ra-tops rocks, yeah,___ Tri-ce-ra-tops

17 | rocks, yeah,___ Tri-ce-ra-tops lock their horns, they

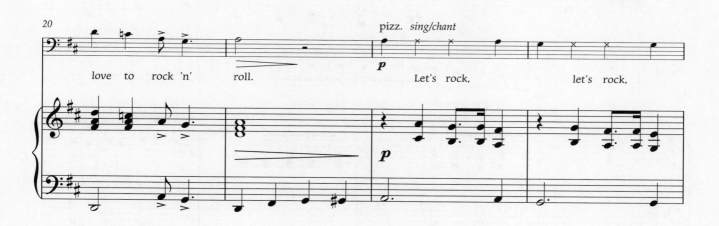

20 | pizz. *sing/chant* | love to rock 'n' roll. Let's rock, let's rock,

poco rit.

24 | arco | let's rock 'n' roll, Tri-ce-ra-tops rocks!___

Dotty Diplodocus

Suggestion box

1 Clap bars 5–12 and 20–27
2 Clap bars 14–17
3 Play each section before putting together

With a good swing ♩ = 104 – 116

Dot - ty Dip - lo-do - cus come and dance with me,⎯ stamp your feet and try to shake your

bo - dy. Dot - ty Dip - lo-do-cus come and dance with me,⎯ hey there,

dance with⎯ me.⎯ I'm free. Come and dance,

Teaching points

- Semitone movement of first finger (E♭–E♮)
- Tap cello with right hand and click with the left

Jurassic Blue

Suggestion box

1 Practise tap and click intro.
2 Practise sliding first finger (as bar 5)
3 Have fun playing!

Groovy marcato ♩ = 108

CELLO TEACHING MATERIAL
FROM FABER MUSIC

PAT LEGG

Superstudies

*Really easy original studies for
the young player*

BOOK 1 ISBN 0-571-51378-6
BOOK 2 ISBN 0-571-51445-6

PAT LEGG and ALAN GOUT

Learning the Tenor Clef

*Progressive Studies and Pieces
for Cellists*

ISBN 0-571-51917-2

MARY COHEN

Superduets

*Fantastic cello duets
for beginners*

BOOK 1 ISBN 0-571-51891-5
BOOK 2 ISBN 0-571-51892-3

PAT LEGG and ALAN GOUT

Thumb Position for
Beginners

*Easy pieces for cello duet
and cello/piano*

ISBN 0-571-51801-X

MARY COHEN

Technique takes off!

*14 intermediate studies
for solo cello*

ISBN 0-571-51420-0

PAT LEGG and ALAN GOUT

Thumb Position Repertoire

*Intermediate pieces
for cello and piano*

ISBN 0-571-51802-8

**POLLY WATERFIELD
and GILLIAN LUBACH**

Polytekniks

*Cello duets for musical and
technical accomplishment*

EASY ISBN 0-571-51490-1
INTERMEDIATE ISBN 0-571-51499-5

PAT LEGG

Position Jazz

*Up-beat, original pieces
for cello duet*

ISBN 0-571-51144-9

FABER *ff* MUSIC

Bony Stegosaurus

on an idea by Matthew

> 1 Sing and place fingers
> 2 Play

Spiky! ♩ = 104
Col legno

Bo -ny Ste - go - sau - rus,

do you think he saw us, is he look - ing at me?

to Coda

Bo - ny Ste - go - sau - rus, what a di - no - sau - rus, don't you think we should

flee? Ar - mour pla - ted back - bone, scares your foes a - way.

D. S. al poi al Coda   CODA

What an ug - ly crea - ture, turn and run a - way.   flee?

Which dinosaur is this?

_____

Clever Compsognatus

1 Sing
2 Play slowly with slurs in twos
3 Play using a bow to a bar
   (once learnt)

Bouncy waltz time ♩ = 112

sing

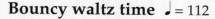

La   la la la la.

arco

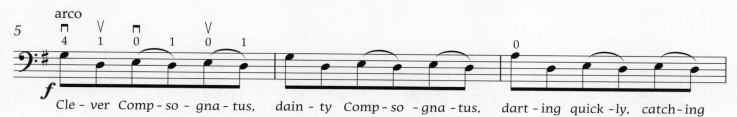

Cle - ver Comp - so - gna - tus,   dain - ty Comp - so - gna - tus,   dart - ing quick - ly, catch - ing

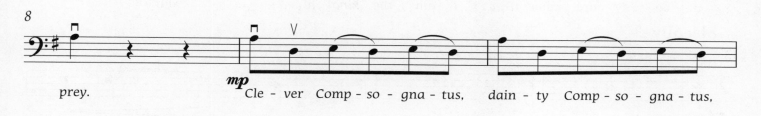

prey.   Cle - ver Comp - so - gna - tus,   dain - ty Comp - so - gna - tus,

don't take fright and run a - way.   We could both be friends, I'd

take you home to tea; come to stay.   Cle - ver Comp - so - gna - tus,

dain - ty comp - so - gna - tus, stay and play.

Lazy Tyrannosaurus Rex

1 Sing
2 Play bars 13–20
3 Play bars 5–12

Relaxed ♩ = 132

Slap shoulder of cello

King di - no - saur, King di - no - saur, King di - no - saur,

Bouncy

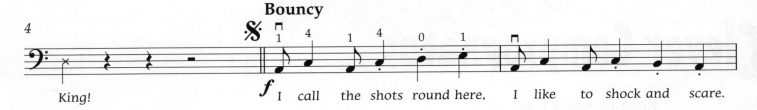

King! *f* I call the shots round here, I like to shock and scare.

Chal - lenge me if you dare, I'm king. *mp* I call the shots round here,

FINE

no - bo - dy dare come near, I am the king di - no - saur.

Sleepily

mf Don't be fooled by slee - py jaws,

D. S. 𝄋 al Fine

p king of all the di - no - saurs.

cresc. *f*

Now try inventing your own dinosaur piece!

𝄢

𝄢

𝄢

Triceratops Rocks

on an idea by Phoebe

1 Sing and clap
2 Learn bars 10–13 and 22–26
3 Play

Dotty Diplodocus

1 Clap bars 5–12 and 20–27
2 Clap bars 14–17
3 Play each section before putting together

Jurassic Blue

1 Practise tap and click intro.
2 Practise sliding first finger
  (as bar 5)
3 Have fun playing!

Groovy marcato ♩ = 108